D1319877

The Art of CHINESE PAPER FOLDING

for Young and Old

WRITTEN AND ILLUSTRATED

by Maying Soong

HARCOURT, BRACE AND COMPANY
NEW YORK

TO JUNIOR AMERICANS

FOREWORD

Chinese are world-renowned for their handicraft. In China, little boys and girls are taught by their elders to use their hands. Even at an early age those chubby hands with their tiny, nimble fingers, are busily engaged in making paper toys such as boats, boxes, hats, and birds, for themselves and their playmates.

This paper-folding art, as we call it in China, is done with only a single sheet of paper and your hands, without any pasting together or the use of scissors. It is the most interesting, inexpensive, and useful art for children and grownups. It gives endless joy to youngsters and also to invalids confined to the narrow limits of a home or hospital. It can be most advantageously used as therapy for patients with paralyzed hands endeavoring to regain their dexterity.

When I was a little girl my mother taught me, as her mother had taught her, how to make toys with paper. I used to spend many rainy days trying to create new objects that neither my mother nor my grandmother knew how to make. I was so proud of myself!

Of course, this was a long time ago. Now I have a little girl of my own. She loves all the things I teach her to make, especially the multicolored ones that we make together for her birthday and Christmas parties. Her little friends, and their parents, all enjoy them as much as we do. They come back time and again to get me to show them how to do the paper objects. Their eagerness and deep interest have prompted me to put my paper

Foreword

foldings in a book.

I hope that my American friends, especially the Junior Americans, will find great interest and enjoyment in the art of paper folding.

MAYING SOONG

CONTENTS

*The contents are grouped under four convenient
headings, and are not arranged chronologically.*

Contents

INTRODUCTION

The different objects in this book are arranged in such a way that the simpler and easier ones are shown in the beginning of the book, while the more elaborate ones appear in the subsequent pages.

Every step is shown by a numbered figure and should be followed in accordance with the accompanying directions.

When dotted lines are shown in the figure it always means to fold the object and leave it folded, unless otherwise stated.

Folding must be accurately done so that corners and edges will meet evenly. Folds should be creased securely to make them stay in place. Usually, it is best to use the pressure of a thumb nail tip to press the fold into place.

When the directions indicate that the paper is to be folded, creased, and *unfolded* before proceeding to the next step, the creases which are indicated by a very fine line in the figure are intended to be used as a guide to keep the work accurate, or as a preparation for the next step.

A square of paper is used for making almost all of the

folded novelties described in this book. On pages x, xi and xii are shown simple methods for making accurate squares.

1. To obtain the largest square from any sized piece of paper:

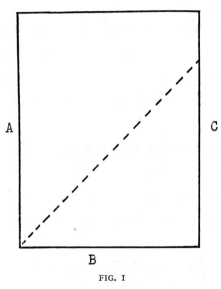

FIG. I

Fold on the dotted line by bringing line B on line A.

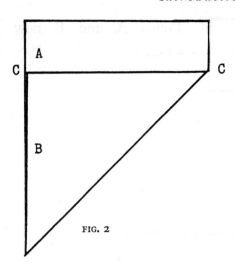

FIG. 2

Cut on line C-C. When unfolded the square is the largest that can be obtained from this piece of paper.

2. To obtain a square of any desired size:

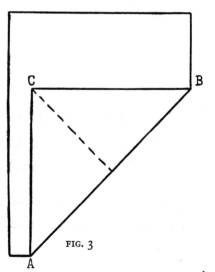

FIG. 3

Make a diagonal fold in a piece of paper that is larger in both length and width than the desired square.

Fold again on dotted line.

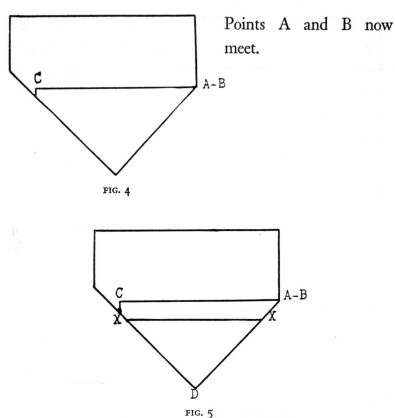

Points A and B now meet.

FIG. 4

FIG. 5

Measure and mark any desired length from point D toward A-B, and use the same length from D toward C. (Line X to X will be the length of a side of the square.)

Cut from point X to X through all folds of the paper. Unfold, and you will have a square of the desired size.

THE ART OF CHINESE PAPER FOLDING
for Young and Old

"LOVE KNOT"

This is a good way to fold an informal letter or note. The "love knot" is specially designed to be used in schools and libraries, and in dormitory mailboxes, where notes are so often exchanged, and where envelopes are a bother.

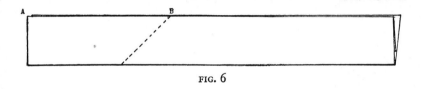

FIG. 6

Write your note on any size of writing paper. Fold the sheet into a long strip as shown in Fig. 6. Then fold on the slanted dotted line, so that line A-B will fall straight as in Fig. 7.

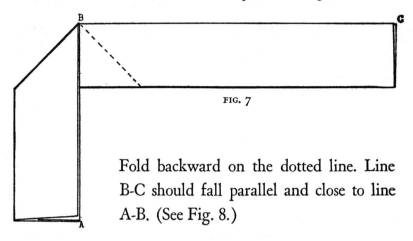

FIG. 7

Fold backward on the dotted line. Line B-C should fall parallel and close to line A-B. (See Fig. 8.)

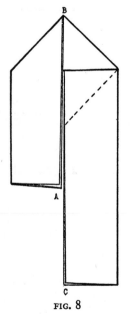

Fold backward on the dotted line.

FIG. 8

4

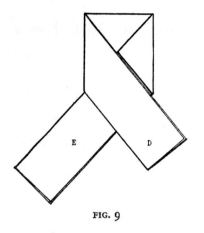

Place leg D behind leg E.

FIG. 9

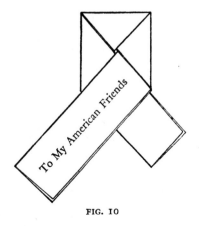

Finished "love knot." Write name on leg E. Now it is ready to deliver your message with love.

FIG. 10

PAPER CUP

How to make a paper cup when you wish to have a drink and no other cup is available.

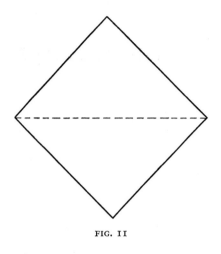

FIG. 11

Place a piece of square paper (8″ x 8″ is a good size) in the position shown in Fig. 11, and fold on the dotted line.

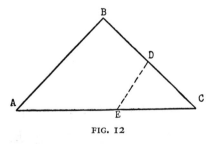

FIG. 12

Bring point C to line A-B so that line C-D is parallel with line A-E. (See Fig. 13.) Fold on dotted line.

Cup now in position Fig. 13.

Turn it over to the other side.

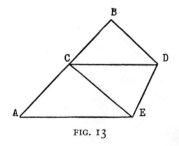

FIG. 13

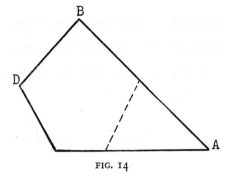

FIG. 14

Bring point A to point D. Crease on dotted line.

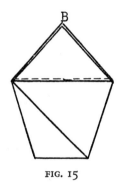

FIG. 15

Fold on the dotted line, bringing upper sheet of point B downward.

Turn cup over and repeat on the other side.

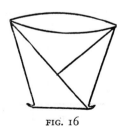

FIG. 16

Finished cup opened at the top; lower corners brought upward to keep it open.

7

DUTCH HAT

To make this hat, paper should be rectangular in shape, its length 1½ times its width. For a child to wear, use paper approximately 17″ x 8½″. It may also be made small enough for a doll.

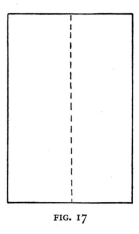

FIG. 17

Fold on the dotted line. Unfold.

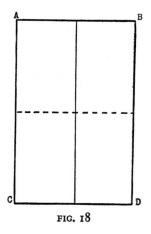

FIG. 18

Fold on the dotted line by bringing line A-B to line C-D.

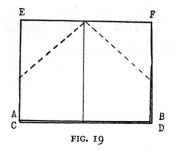

FIG. 19

Fold on the dotted lines so that point E and point F meet at the center line.

Fold on the dotted line, bringing line A-B upward.

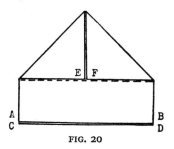

FIG. 20

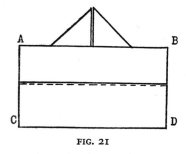

FIG. 21

Turn the hat over to the other side and bring line C-D upward, folding on the dotted line.

Finished hat, opened at the bottom and ready to be worn.

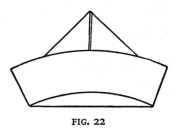

FIG. 22

9

This bird can be made nicely with writing paper. Tissue or heavy paper will not serve the purpose.

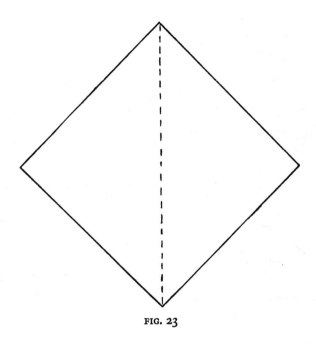

Take a piece of square paper (6″ x 6″) and place it as in Fig. 23.

Fold on the dotted line. Crease, and unfold.

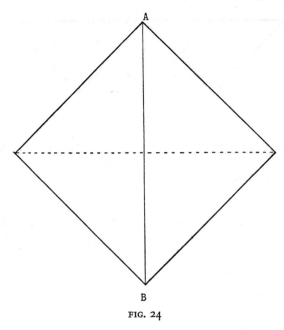

FIG. 24

Bring point A to point B and fold on the dotted line.

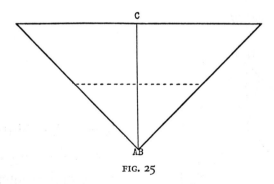

FIG. 25

Bring point AB to point C and fold on the dotted line.

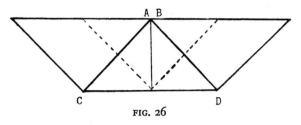

FIG. 26

Fold on dotted lines by bringing point D to AB and point C to AB.

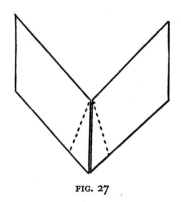

FIG. 27

Fold on the dotted lines. Crease, and unfold.

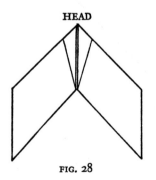

HEAD

FIG. 28

Turn the bird upside down. Push up the head through the center. Crease well.

12

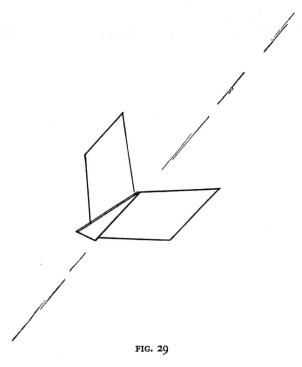

FIG. 29

Finished bird that will fly when thrown from the fingers. To fly this bird, hold its head between your index and middle finger. Lift your hand up high and throw the bird off with a little swing. It can fly gracefully for some distance.

13

DUSTPAN

Little girls can use a miniature dustpan when they are playing house.

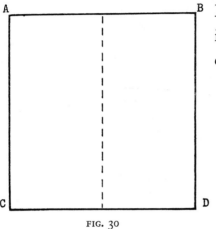

FIG. 30

Fold a square of paper, 8 inches or smaller, on the dotted line. Unfold.

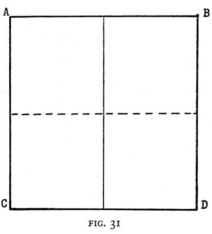

FIG. 31

Fold on dotted line, bringing line A-B to line C-D.

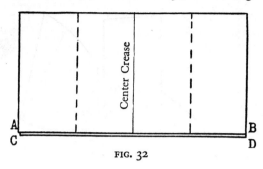

FIG. 32

Fold on the dotted lines, bringing points AC and BD together at the center crease.

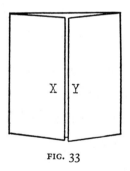

FIG. 33

Folded paper now looks as in Fig. 33.

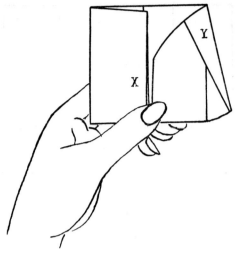

FIG. 34

Study Fig. 34 before proceeding.

Slip left thumb inside Y, and holding underside firmly in place with thumb, pull upperside all of the way out to the right. Crease on the diagonal lines at the top. (See Fig. 35.) Repeat with X.

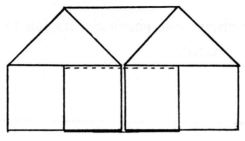

FIG. 35

Fold on the dotted line upward.

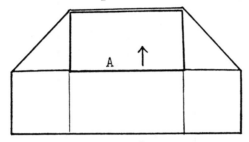

FIG. 36

Open dustpan by pushing line A up.

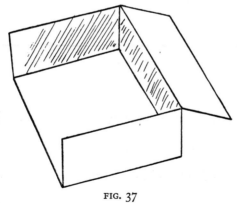

FIG. 37

Finished dustpan.

Children always love pinwheels. It's fun to be able to make them yourself.

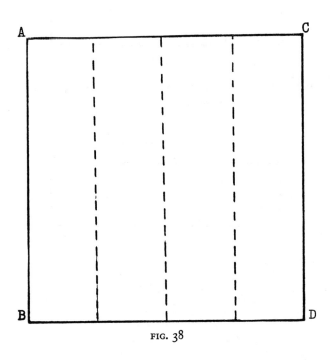

FIG. 38

Fold a square approximately 8½″ down the middle. Crease. Unfold.

Bring lines A-B and C-D to center crease line. Fold.

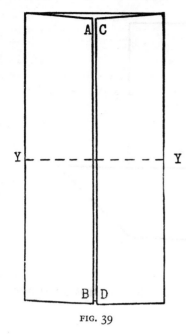

FIG. 39

Fold on the dotted line Y-Y. Crease. Unfold.

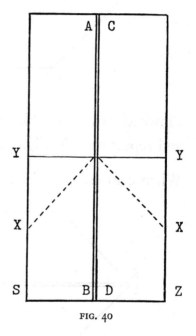

FIG. 40

Pick up lower corner D and lift upward to right, matching edge (line C-D) with creased line Y. Fold across diagonal dotted line.

Repeat with lower corner B, lifting it upward toward left and folding.

Fold underside from X to X and crease flat.

19

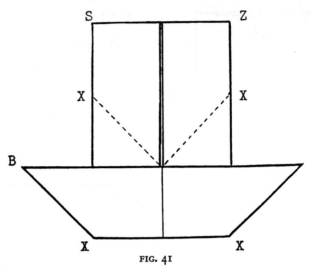

FIG. 41

Pinwheel now looks like Fig. 41. Turn it upside down and repeat steps in Fig. 40.

When completed model will look as in Fig. 42.

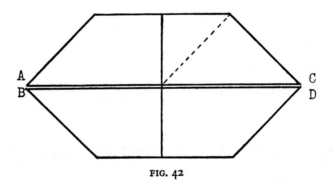

FIG. 42

Bring point C upward by folding on the dotted line.

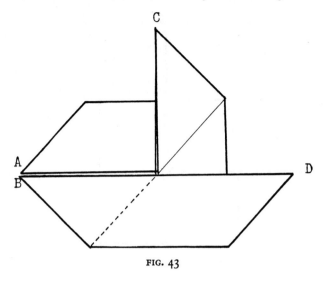

FIG. 43

Fold on the dotted line by bringing point B downward.

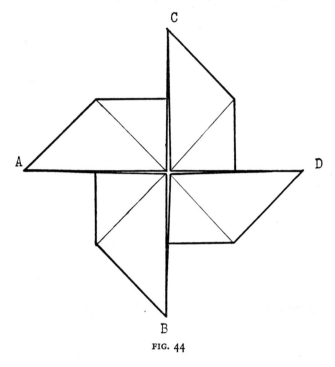

FIG. 44

Folded pinwheel.

Cut two small ½″ squares. Paste one over the center to catch the corners together. Stick a pin through the center of the pinwheel, then through the center of the second small square, and then push it firmly into a stick.

Pull the flaps of the pinwheel open, and it is ready for a whirl in the breeze.

22

SMALL BOX

Boxes are always useful for children's collections. Heavy writing or wrapping paper will be most suitable to make the box.

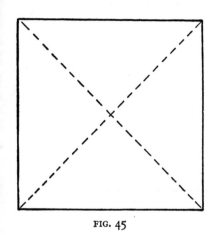

FIG. 45

Fold a square of paper diagonally on the dotted lines. Crease. Unfold.

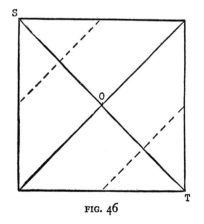

FIG. 46

Fold and crease on the dotted lines by bringing corners S and T to center O. Unfold.

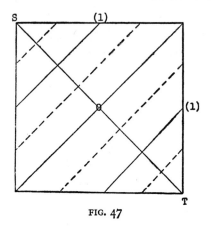

FIG. 47

Bring point S to crease (1), then fold by rolling over again and again on the dotted lines until fold meets center O.

Repeat with point T.

When this step is finished it should look like Fig. 48.

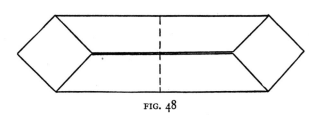

FIG. 48

Fold to the back at dotted line.

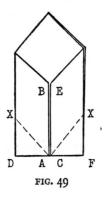

FIG. 49

Fold on the dotted lines by bringing line A-B on line A-D, and line C-E on line C-F, creasing on diagonal line. Then crease across points X.

When finished turn Fig. 49 over and place it in position Fig. 50.

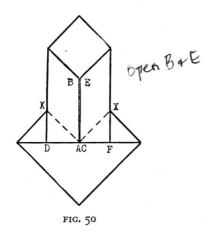

open B + E

FIG. 50

Repeat steps in Fig. 49 to Fig. 50.

Fold upper section on dotted lines so that points P meet at center line.

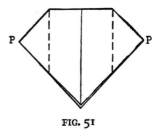

FIG. 51

25

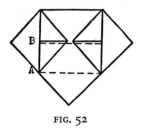

FIG. 52

First fold at dotted line A, then turn over again at dotted line B.

When the above is done, turn Fig. 52 over and repeat steps in Fig. 51 and Fig. 52 on other side.

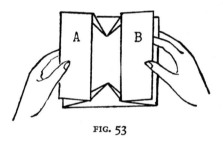

FIG. 53

Open box by pulling flaps A and B apart with thumbs and index fingers while supporting bottom of box with other fingers.

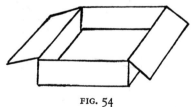

FIG. 54

Finished box.

ROW BOAT

This row boat made of waxed paper, cellophane, or other waterproof paper will float in water for a long time.

Matchsticks and toothpicks can be used in the smaller boats for seats and oars, and to make them look lifelike.

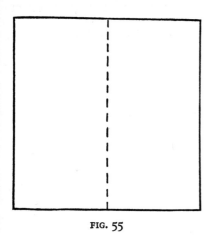

Fold a square in half and crease.

Unfold.

FIG. 55

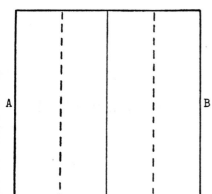

Bring lines A and B to center fold and crease.

FIG. 56

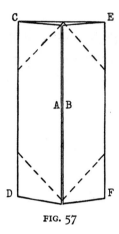

FIG. 57

Fold on diagonal dotted lines, bringing points C, D, E and F to the center line and crease.

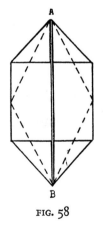

FIG. 58

Fold on dotted lines.

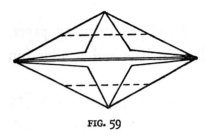

Fold again on dotted lines.

FIG. 59

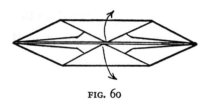

Turn boat inside out, holding folds carefully to prevent tearing.

FIG. 60

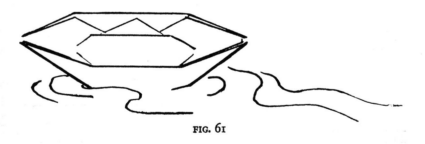

FIG. 61

Finished boat, ready for the bathtub sailor.

NAVY CAP

This hat can be made of colored gift-wrapping paper. Children enjoy making their own hats and it adds fun to parties.

Paper should be rectangular in shape, its length 1½ times its width. For a child's hat, use paper approximately 21″ x 14″.

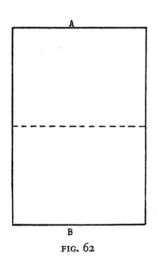

FIG. 62

Fold paper on the dotted line, bringing line A to B.

Fold on lines 1 and 2, crease and unfold.

Fold on the diagonal dotted lines.

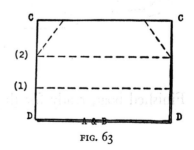

FIG. 63

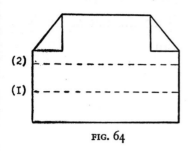

FIG. 64

Fold the upper sheet on the dotted lines, folding first on line (1), then rolling over again to crease on line (2). When done, turn Fig. 64 over.

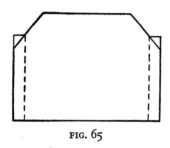

FIG. 65

Fold on the dotted lines. Crease well.

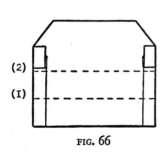

FIG. 66

Fold this side on lines (1) and (2), as in Fig. 64. When completed, tuck ends at top securely into each end of the folded band to hold it in place.

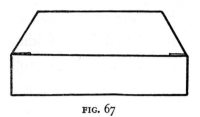

FIG. 67

Open the hat at the bottom.

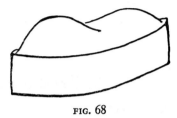

FIG. 68

Completed hat, ready to wear.

PAPER BALL

Paper balls make attractive Christmas tree ornaments when made of shiny, colored papers, or with cellophane. They also can be used as party favors and decorations.

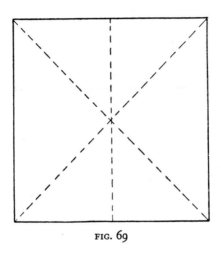

FIG. 69

Take a square of paper, fold, and crease on the dotted lines. Unfold.

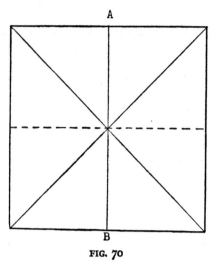

FIG. 70

Fold on the dotted line, bringing A to B.

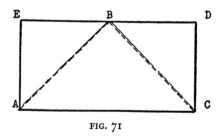

FIG. 71

Fold on the dotted lines by pushing triangles C B D, and A B E *into* triangle A B C. Hold paper in hand as illustrated in Fig. 72.

34

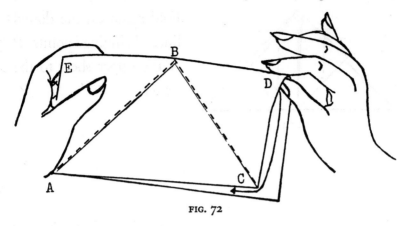

FIG. 72

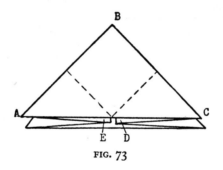

FIG. 73

Fold upper sheet on the dotted lines, bringing point A and point C to point B.

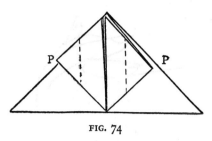

FIG. 74

Fold again on the dotted lines, bringing points P of the upper sheet to the center.

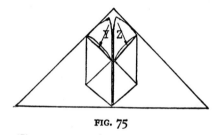

FIG. 75

Tuck flaps Y and Z into the two pockets shown by the arrows until they are even and smooth. Crease.

These flaps will have to be pushed into the pockets.

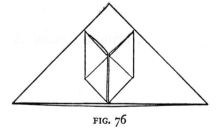

FIG. 76

Turn Fig. 76 over and repeat steps in Figs. 73, 74 and 75.

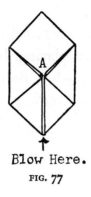

Blow Here.

FIG. 77

Fill the ball with air by blowing into the small hole in the end.

Hold the ball by putting the index fingers of both hands against corners A and touching the outer crease with thumbs and fingers. This will prevent the ball from unfolding as it expands.

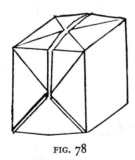

FIG. 78

Finished ball.

37

CHINESE KNIGHT'S HELMET

The knight's helmet will add another hat to the variety that children love to wear when playing. It is not difficult to fold, but looks quite fancy when finished. If you wish a hat in two colors, use two different-colored squares, placed on top of each other, and treat them as a single square.

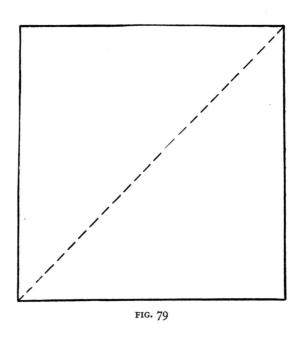

FIG. 79

Fold a piece of square paper diagonally on the dotted line. For a child's hat, use paper approximately 22″ square.

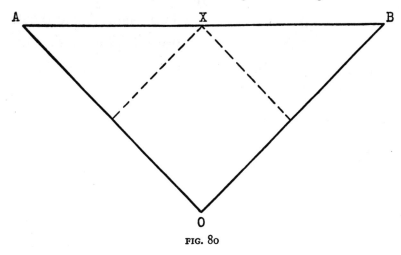

FIG. 80

Place the paper in position as in Fig. 80. Fold on the dotted lines, bringing points A and B to point O.

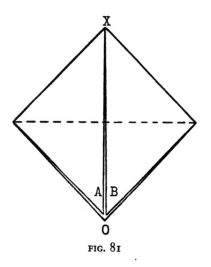

FIG. 81

Bring A and B to point X. Crease on dotted line. Point O stays in position.

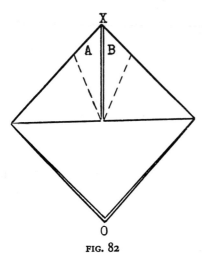

FIG. 82

Turn points A and B outward, folding on the dotted lines of Fig. 82 to make Fig. 83.

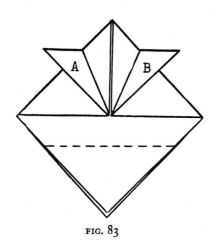

FIG. 83

Fold top sheet upward on dotted line.

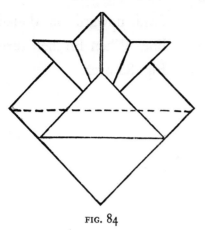

FIG. 84

Fold upper sheet upward again on dotted line. Turn hat (Fig. 84) over to other side.

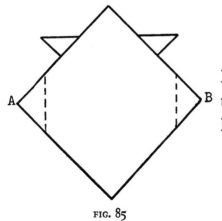

FIG. 85

Fold points A and B toward center on dotted lines.

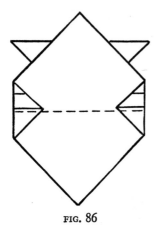

FIG. 86

Fold upward on dotted line. When finished turn Fig. 86 over.

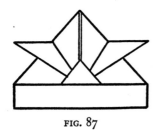

FIG. 87

Open hat at bottom.

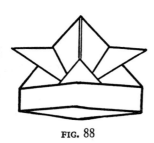

FIG. 88

Completed Chinese knight's helmet.

Fishing boat with awnings. Be sure to crease each fold firmly so that the finished boat will turn inside out easily. If waterproofed paper is used, this boat will float.

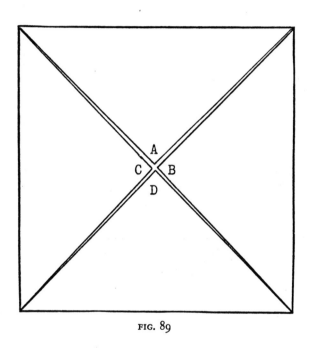

FIG. 89

Follow directions for Figs. 115 and 116 to get illustration, Fig. 89.

Do not turn figure over as stated in directions for Fig. 116.

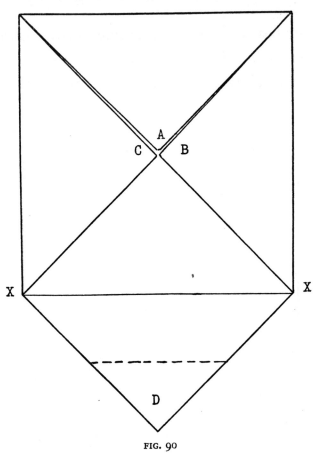

FIG. 90

Fold on the dotted line, bringing point D to line X-X.
Fold over again on line X-X.

44

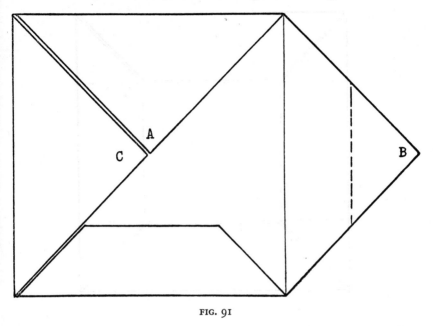

FIG. 91

Repeat directions in Fig. 90 for points A, B and C. When all four sides are done, you should have Fig. 92.

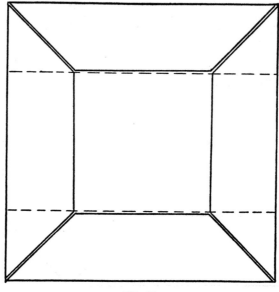

FIG. 92

Fold toward the back, on the dotted lines.

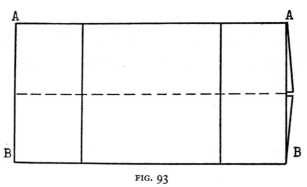

FIG. 93

Place paper in position shown in Fig. 93.

Fold on the dotted line, bringing line A-A to line B-B.

46

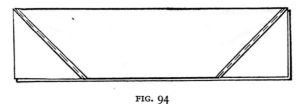

FIG. 94

The boat now looks as in Fig. 94. Fold the upper layer on the dotted lines and crease.

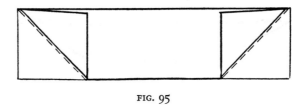

FIG. 95

Fold the lower layer toward the back on the dotted lines.

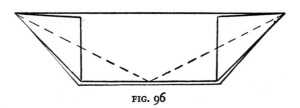

FIG. 96

Fold the upper layer on the dotted lines.

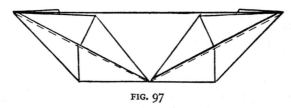

FIG. 97

Fold the lower layer toward the back on the dotted lines.

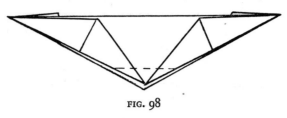

FIG. 98

Fold the top layer upward and the lower layer backward on dotted line.

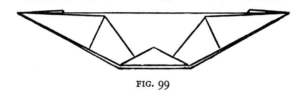

FIG. 99

Boat is now in position, Fig. 99.

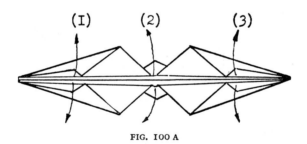

FIG. 100 A

Place boat in floating position. Turn boat inside out carefully, holding all folds tightly in place to prevent loosening. You can do it in three steps (1), (2), and (3), respectively, as shown by the arrows. Study holding in Fig. 100 B.

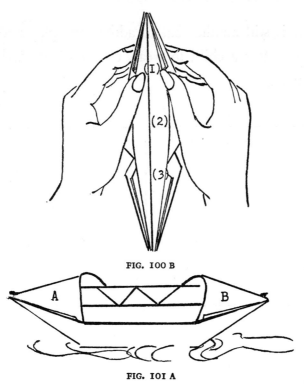

FIG. 100 B

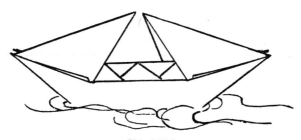

FIG. 101 A

View of finished boat on a sunny day. For rainy weather, pull out under layer of A and B, Fig. 101 A.

FIG. 101 B

View of finished boat on a rainy day.

"OLD SCHOLAR" HAT

Here is still another hat to add to the play and party collection. For a child to wear, use paper approximately 20″ square.

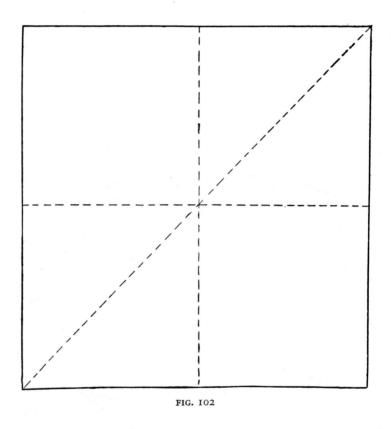

FIG. 102

Fold a square on the dotted lines as in Fig. 102. Crease. Unfold.

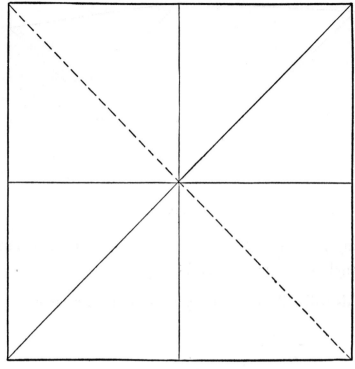

FIG. 103

Fold on the dotted line.

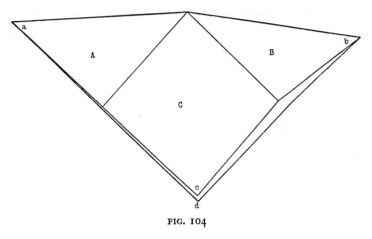

FIG. 104

Bring points b and a *between* points c and d by pushing triangle B and triangle A into square C.

Folds will fall easily on previously formed creases.

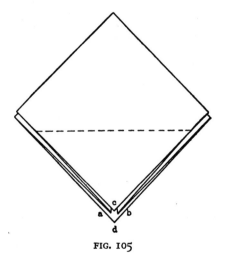

FIG. 105

Bring point c up, folding on dotted line. (Upper sheet only.)

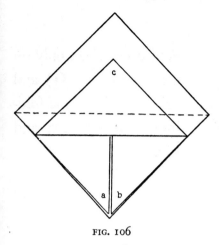

Fold again on dotted line.

FIG. 106

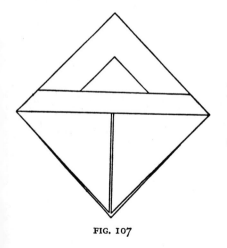

Hat now in position Fig. 107. Turn it over on the other side.

FIG. 107

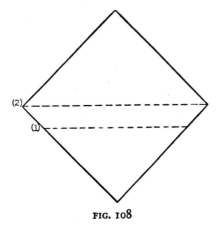

FIG. 108

Fold upper sheet only on the dotted lines (1) and (2), repeating same folding as in Fig. 105 and Fig. 106.

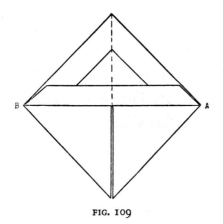

FIG. 109

Fold on dotted line, bringing point A to point B.

Repeat same on back.

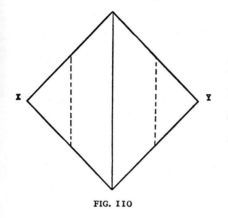

FIG. 110

Fold upper layer on dotted lines so that points X and Y will meet on the center line.

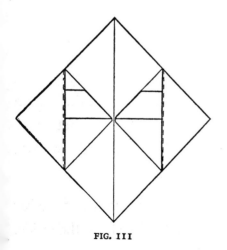

FIG. 111

Repeat, folding lower layer toward back on the dotted lines.

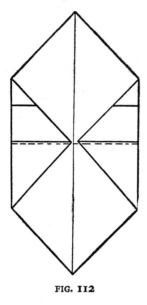

FIG. 112

Fold on the dotted line, bringing the upper layer toward the front, the lower layer toward the back.

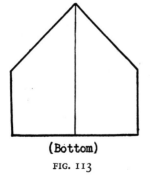

(Bottom)

FIG. 113

Open the hat by pulling apart gently at the bottom of the flaps that were folded upward in Fig. 112.

Ease the crown of the hat into place from the inside.

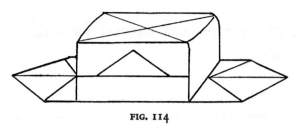

FIG. 114

Completed Ming Dynasty officer's hat for a would-be officer.

FOOTSTOOL

Little girls can make a footstool for their own doll house furniture.

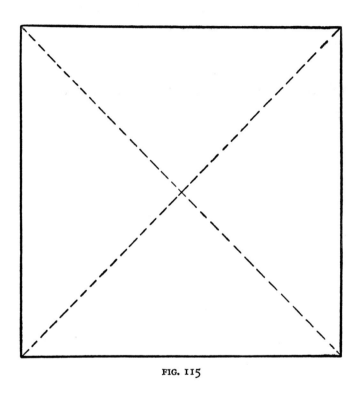

FIG. 115

Use a square piece of paper (any size desired). Fold and crease on the dotted lines.

Unfold.

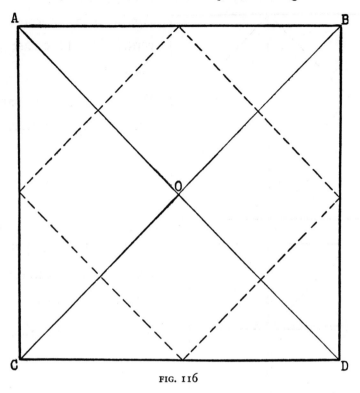

FIG. 116

Bring points A, B, C and D to center point O. Crease on dotted lines.

When finished turn Fig. 116 over to the other side.

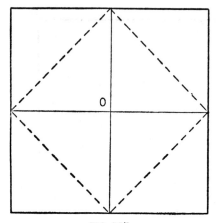

FIG. 117

Again bring corners to center O and crease on the dotted lines.

When done, turn paper over to the other side.

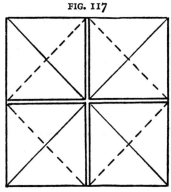

FIG. 118

Fold on the dotted lines, bringing corners to center again, and crease.

Turn to the other side.

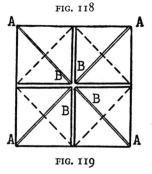

FIG. 119

Open each corner square by bringing point B to point A (opening and spreading upper layer outward, as in Fig. 120).

Crease on the dotted lines.

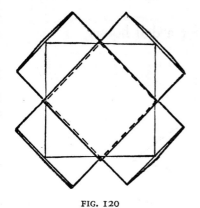

FIG. 120

Fold toward the back on the dotted lines.

Crease firmly, pressing tightly before releasing.

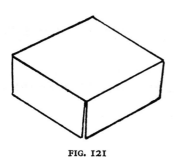

FIG. 121

Release edges and adjust legs in place, and you have a footstool.

CHAIR

Another piece of furniture for a doll house.

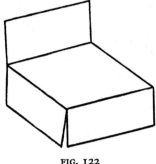

FIG. 122

Repeat the directions for the footstool, Figs. 115, 116, 117, 118, 119 and 120.

When following directions for Fig. 120, fold three sides backward and one side forward.

This will give the chair a back.

This coaster can be made with colored paper to fit in with any color scheme for party table decorations. Its points come up around the base of the glass like petals, which makes it very attractive.

Use a seven-inch square of paper for an ordinary eight-ounce glass coaster.

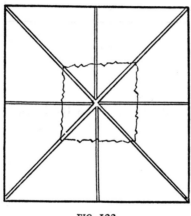

FIG. 123

Follow directions in Figs. 115, 116 and 117 to get illustration Fig. 123. (Do not turn Fig. 117 over.)

Fasten the corners in the center with a small piece of Scotch tape. Coaster is now in position shown in Fig. 123.

Turn paper over to the other side.

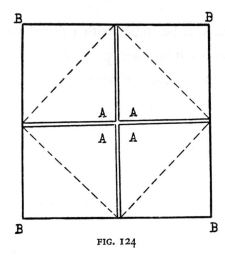

FIG. 124

Fold and crease on dotted lines by bringing points A to points B.

FIG. 125

Finished coaster.

Adjust the petals so they stand up gracefully.

POKE BONNET

Little girls always look attractive in poke bonnets. Here is a model you can make in a few minutes.

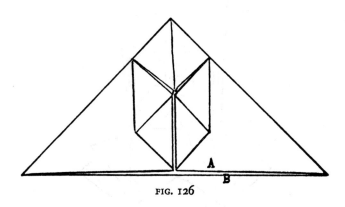

FIG. 126

Use a 24-inch square of pastel crepe paper (other paper can also be used) for a child's bonnet.

Follow Figs. 69, 70, 71, 72, 73, 74 and 75 to get the illustration Fig. 126.

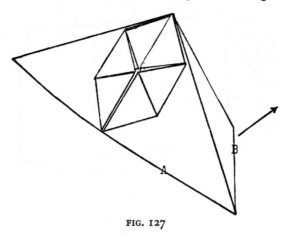

FIG. 127

To open, hold Fig. 127 with left fingers. Pull carefully outward with right fingers at point B, then insert right fingers inside bonnet and push outward until crown is completely opened at back.

When finished it should look like Fig. 128.

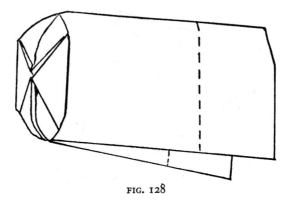

FIG. 128

Fold on dotted line to make a cuff for the bonnet.

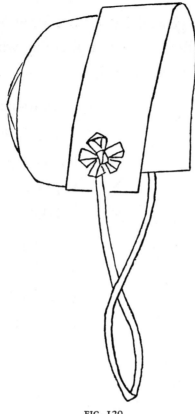

FIG. 129

Decorate the finished bonnet with contrasting colored bows and streamers of crepe paper.

If paper is cut with the grain it will tie in bows without stretching.

It will look even nicer if you decorate the bonnet with real ribbons.

TENT

The amateur general can lay out a camp for his army of tin soldiers. Row on row of gleaming white tents lend importance to his battles.

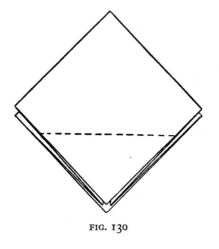

FIG. 130

Use a 10-inch square piece of paper, or larger.

Follow Figs. 102, 103 and 104 to get the illustration Fig. 130.

Fold top sheet only on the dotted line and crease.

When finished turn Fig. 130 over to the other side.

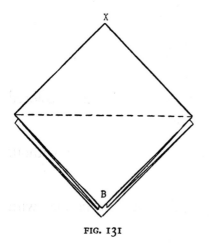

FIG. 131

Fold and crease on the dotted line by bringing point B to point X.

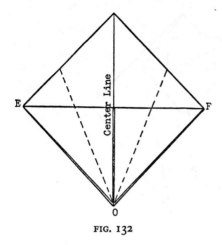

FIG. 132

Bring line E-O and line F-O of upper sheet to center line. Crease on dotted lines.

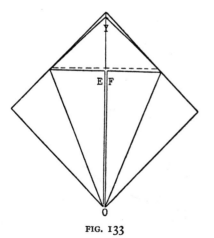

FIG. 133

Fold upper sheet only on the dotted line, bringing corner Y downward.

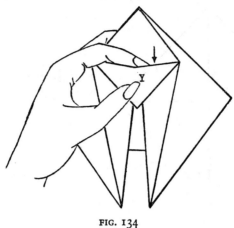

FIG. 134

To open, hold firmly with left thumb on flap Y, and index finger inside pocket shown by arrow.

Insert right fingers in tent and push carefully until completely opened.

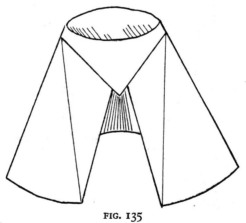

FIG. 135

Completed tent.

EASTER SURPRISE BUNNY

The bunny will add an extra bit of delight to an Easter party. You can even push jelly beans into him through his mouth, if you do it carefully.

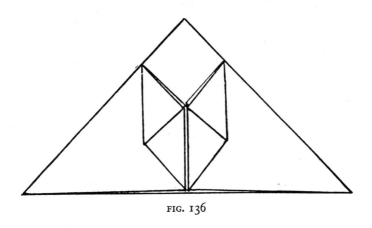

FIG. 136

Use a square piece of paper of any desired size.

Follow the directions in Figs. 69, 70, 71, 72, 73, 74 and 75 to get the illustration in Fig. 136.

Turn Fig. 136 to the other side.

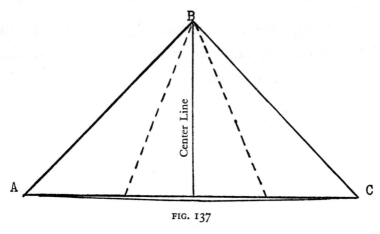

FIG. 137

Bring line A-B and line C-B to center line, and crease on dotted lines.

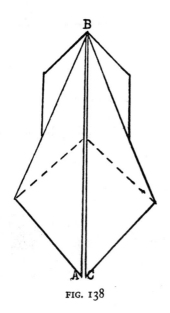

FIG. 138

Fold and crease on the dotted lines.

74

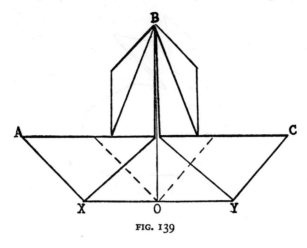

FIG. 139

Fold and crease on the dotted lines by bringing line X-O and line Y-O to center line O-B.

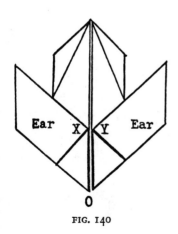

FIG. 140

Open bunny by placing index finger of left hand on point X-Y. Lift ears up and hold them each side of index finger, with thumb and first finger.

Blow at point O.

FIG. 141

Finished bunny.

(Draw eyes and whiskers with pencil, if you wish.)

STEAMBOATS

These boats won't float—but the captains and crews of little boys' parties will approve the paper Navy.

Use an 8-inch square of paper (preferably gray color) for the first boat and smaller size paper for the boats in the distance.

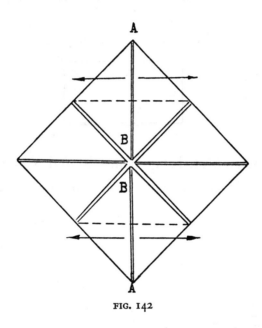

FIG. 142

Follow Figs. 115, 116, 117 and 118 to get illustration, Fig. 142.

Open upper and lower squares by bringing points B to points A (opening and spreading upper layers outward).

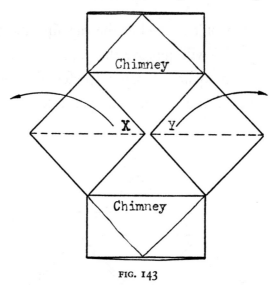

FIG. 143

To open steamboat, bring points X and Y upward and outward—and at the same time bringing the chimneys together.

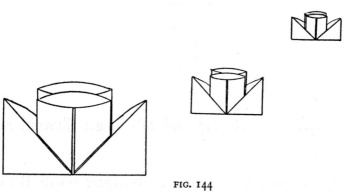

FIG. 144

Finished steamboats.

WINGED HAT

Another hat to add to the variety for parties.

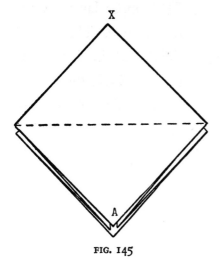

FIG. 145

Use a 24-inch square for a child's hat.

Follow directions for Figs. 102, 103 and 104 to get illustration Fig. 145.

Bring point A to point X and crease on the dotted line.

Turn to other side and repeat.

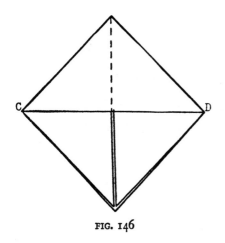

FIG. 146

Fold on the dotted line, bringing point C to point D.

Turn to the other side and repeat.

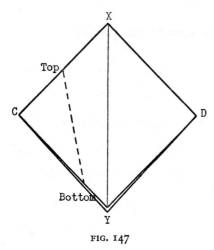

FIG. 147

Fold upper layer on the dotted line. The top of the dotted line is halfway between C-X; the bottom is one third of the distance between C-Y.

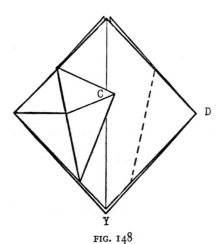

FIG. 148

Fold on the dotted line. Note that corners C and D overlap each other.

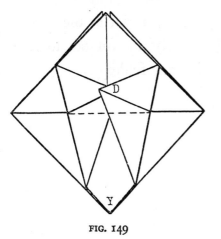

FIG. 149

Fold on the dotted line upward.

Crease.

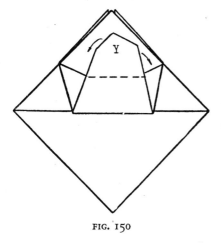

FIG. 150

Fold on the dotted line, tucking flap Y behind points C and D. (Figs. 148 and 149.)

Turn to the other side and repeat directions for Figs. 147, 148, 149 and 150.

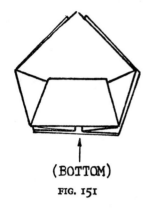

Open hat at the bottom. (Be careful not to undo any foldings.)

(BOTTOM)

FIG. 151

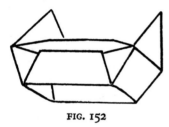

FIG. 152

Finished winged hat.

CANDY AND PLACE CARD BASKET

This candy basket can be made very attractive with colored papers to fit into any party scheme. A name can be written on each of these baskets as they are being folded so that they can also serve as place cards.

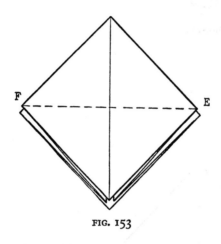

FIG. 153

Use an 8″ square of paper and follow the directions for Figs. 102, 103 and 104 to get illustration Fig. 153.

Fold all layers together on the dotted lines. Crease and unfold.

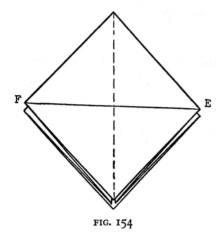

FIG. 154

Bring point E (top layer only) to the left on F.

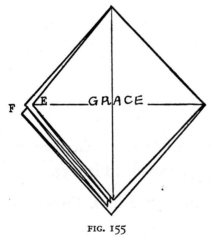

FIG. 155

Add name, centering it by using creased guide lines.

Return point E to its former position (as in Fig. 153).

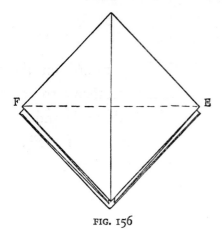

FIG. 156

Fold (top sheet only) on the dotted line.

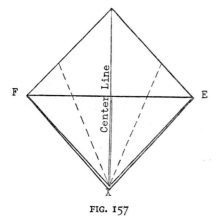

FIG. 157

Bring lines X-F and X-F (top layer only) to center line.

Fold on the dotted lines.

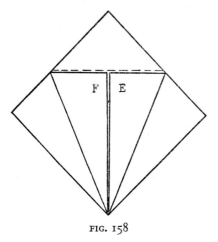

FIG. 158

Fold downward on the
dotted line, then turn Fig.
158 to other side and re-
peat directions for Figs.
156, 157 and 158.

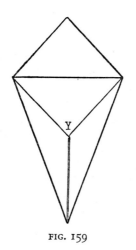

FIG. 159

To open, hold both sides
at flap Y, and pull apart.

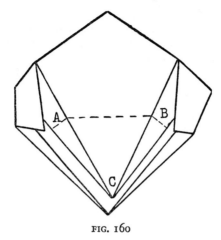

FIG. 160

Fold on the dotted line, pushing triangle A B C to the inside.

Repeat the above directions on the other side.

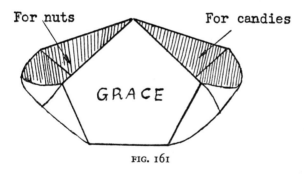

FIG. 161

Finished candy and place card basket.

LIGHTHOUSE BOOKMARK

Every reader likes to have a nice bookmark. Here is one that you can make. Write your favorite motto on it.

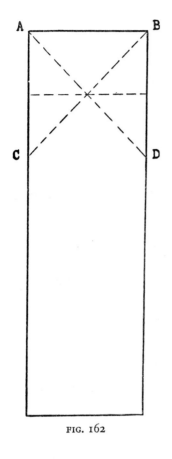

FIG. 162

Cut a piece of paper 8 inches long and 2½ inches wide.

Fold on the dotted lines by bringing line A-B to line B-D, crease and unfold: line A-B to line A-C, crease and unfold: line A-B to line C-D, crease and unfold.

To get Fig. 163, follow directions for Figs. 69, 70, 71 and 72.

FIG. 163

To get Fig. 164, follow the directions for Figs. 182, 183, 184, 185 and 186.

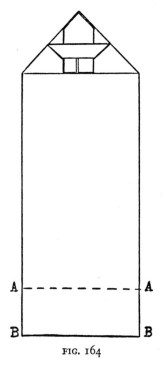

FIG. 164

Fold on dotted line A-A, about one inch from base.

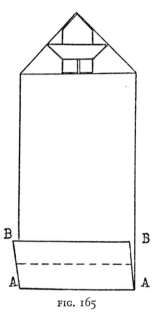

Fold on the dotted line, bringing line B-B to line A-A.

FIG. 165

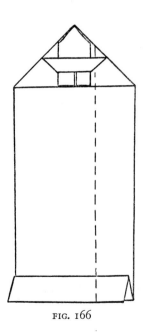

Fold backward on the dotted line, approximately one-third of the width.

Turn paper over to the other side.

FIG. 166

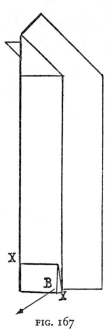

FIG. 167

Pull corner B down toward the left, creasing on a line from points X to X.

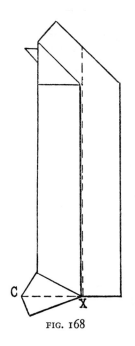

FIG. 168

Cut on dotted line C-X, then fold at the lengthwise dotted line and pull lower corner down, as in Fig. 167, but toward the right side, and cut.

When finished, turn Fig. 168 over.

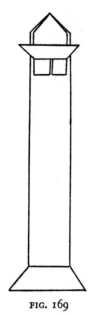

The lighthouse bookmark is ready for your favorite proverb or motto.

FIG. 169

MONKEY

This is another toy that you can make yourself and have lots of fun.

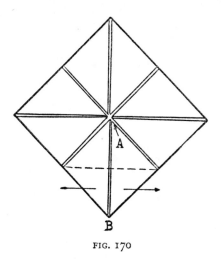

FIG. 170

To get Fig. 170, follow the directions for Figs. 115, 116, 117 and 118.

Bring point A to point B by opening square and folding on dotted line.

Pull corner Y all the way up and out to the right. This will include unfolding all of the right side on the back as well.

Paper now in position as illustrated in Fig. 172.

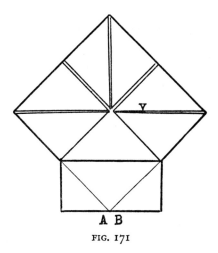

FIG. 171

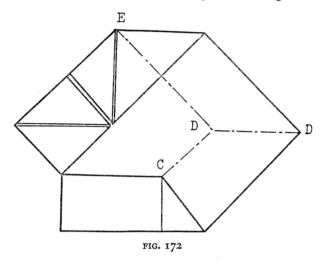

FIG. 172

Fold backward on dotted line C-D; almost at the same time fold backward on dotted line E-DD.

Repeat directions for Fig. 171 and Fig. 172 to left side of paper.

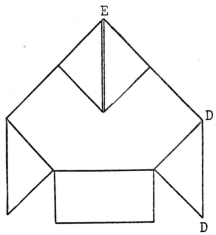

It now appears as illustrated in Fig. 173.

Turn it over to the other side (front side).

(Back side)

FIG. 173

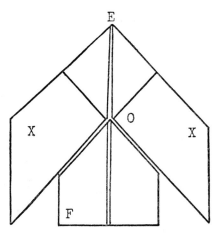

(Front side)

FIG. 174

Place index finger of left hand against point O, and bring parts X toward each other with thumb and first finger. (See Fig. 175.)

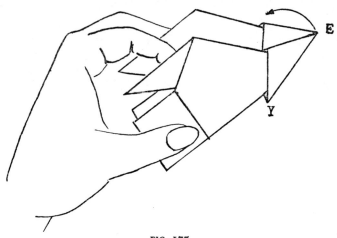

FIG. 175

It is being held in left hand as shown in Fig. 175. Then, with right index finger push frontward on E. At same time use right thumb to bring Y upward.

Note position of Y and E in Fig. 176.

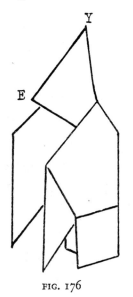

FIG. 176

Side view of finished monkey. Eyes and mouth may be added with pencil. It can stand by itself.

The bird is one of the most amusing objects. Its wings can be made to flap.

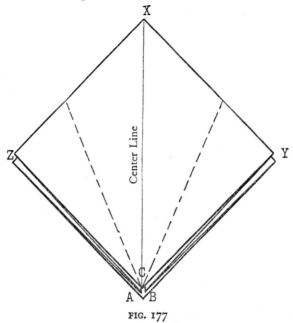

FIG. 177

Use a square piece of paper, any size desired.

Follow the directions for Figs. 102, 103 and 104 to get illustration in Fig. 177.

Bring line C-Z and C-Y to center line. Crease on the dotted lines. Unfold.

Turn Fig. 177 over to the other side and repeat the above directions.

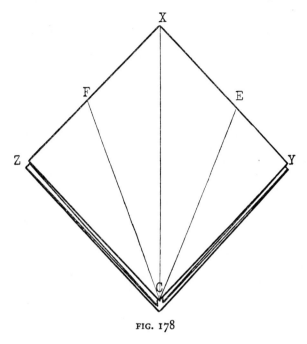

FIG. 178

Push triangle C Y E inside triangle C E X and fold on the creased line C-E.

Push triangle C Z F inside triangle C F X and fold on the creased line C-F.

Turn it over to the other side and repeat the above directions.

When finished on both sides, model appears as illustrated in Fig. 179.

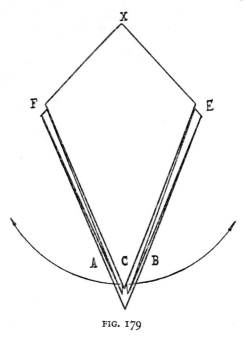

FIG. 179

Bring point B out and up, reversing the crease down its center as it is being pulled out. Bring it up into position at an angle as indicated in Fig. 180. Before creasing it into position, examine edges inside. They must be flat and smooth the whole length of the crease, especially at the center of the bird.

Repeat the above directions with point A.

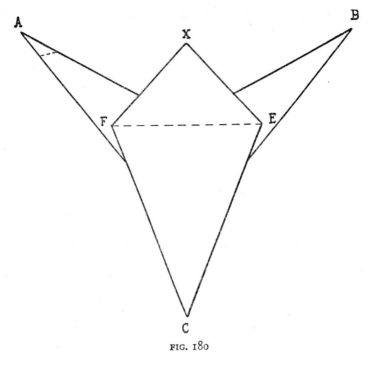

FIG. 180

The head of the bird is made by reversing the crease at the tip of point A and folding on the dotted line indicated there.

The wings are brought into position by bringing point C upward and creasing on the dotted line E-F. Repeat same directions on the reverse side.

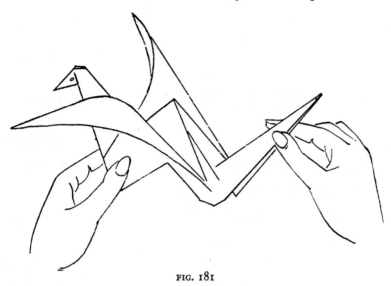

FIG. 181

Finished bird.

Hold it in position as in Fig. 181. Pull and push the tail in and out to make the wings flap.

You will need nine squares to make this intricate bookmark. It is especially attractive when made from glossy paper of different colors.

Each flight is made separately, and inserted one into the other according to size.

Perfect cutting of the squares, and careful folding, is necessary to make this model successfully. It is not difficult, but the work must be exact.

The squares are cut to size as follows: $3\frac{1}{2}''$; $3\frac{1}{4}''$; $3''$; $2\frac{3}{4}''$; $2\frac{1}{2}''$; $2\frac{1}{4}''$; $2''$; $1\frac{3}{4}''$ and $1\frac{1}{2}''$. It will be noted that they graduate from $3\frac{1}{2}''$ to $1\frac{1}{2}''$ with $\frac{1}{4}''$ difference in size between each square.

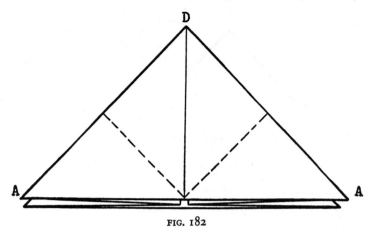

FIG. 182

Begin with the 3½″ square which will become the bottom flight.

To get Fig. 182, follow directions for Figs. 69, 70, 71 and 72.

Bring points A to point D. Crease on the dotted lines.

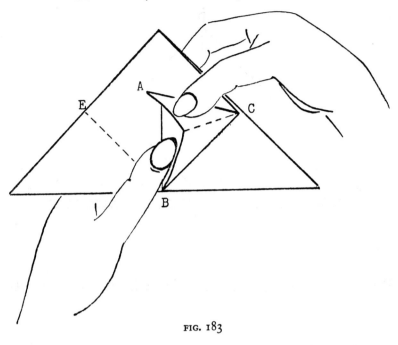

FIG. 183

Hold paper in position Fig. 183. (Put left thumb inside triangle A B C.) Use right thumb to push line C-A down until triangle A B C opens into a square.

Reverse your hand position and repeat same directions to the left side of Fig. 183.

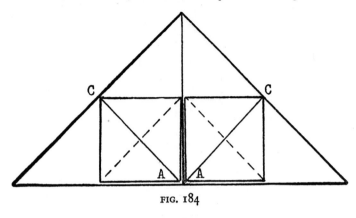

FIG. 184

Fold on dotted lines by bringing points A to points C.

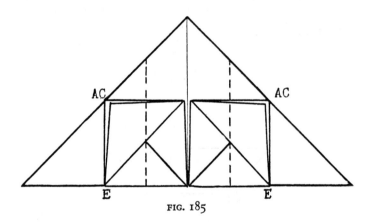

FIG. 185

It is now in position illustrated in Fig. 185.

Fold top layer toward back on dotted lines, turning edges E-AC to inside. Crease on each side.

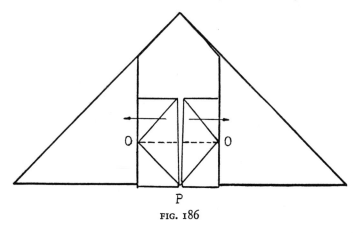

FIG. 186

Open the lines apart to left and right as indicated by the arrows in Fig. 186, and at the same time bring point P upward and fold across line O-O.

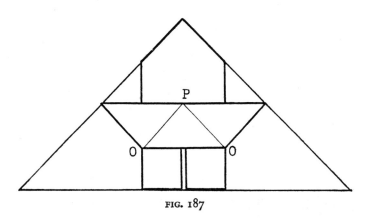

FIG. 187

Turn it (Fig. 187) over to other side and repeat directions for Figs. 182, 183, 184, 185 and 186.

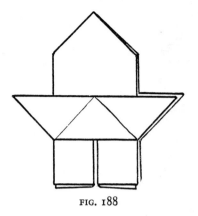

FIG. 188

Finished first flight (Fig. 188).

Repeat the above directions from Fig. 182 to Fig. 187 on the other eight flights.

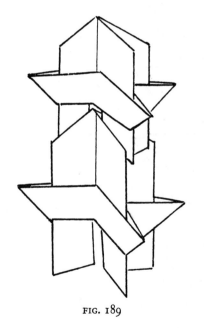

FIG. 189

Attach the flights together by slipping the two legs of the smaller flight into the grooves of the next larger crown.

Push into place until the peak of the crown slides out of sight.

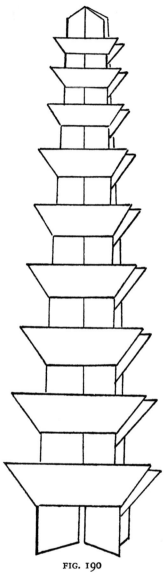

FIG. 190

Finished pagoda bookmark.

FLOWERED CANDY BOX

This is an attractive and practical box which can be made with a single sheet of paper. It may serve as an individual candy box on tables at Christmas parties, etc.

A rectangular piece of paper consisting of two equal squares is used to make this box. 4″ x 8″ is a good size for the above purpose.

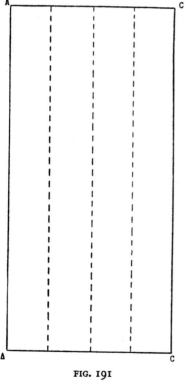

Fold on the center dotted line and crease. Unfold, then bring lines A-A and C-C to center crease, and fold.

FIG. 191

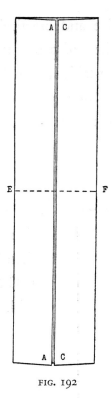

FIG. 192

Fold toward the back, on dotted line E-F.

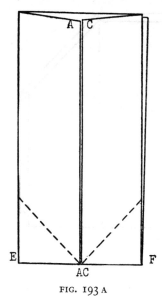

FIG. 193 A

Bring line C-C on line C-F by creasing on dotted line.

Repeat on left side, bringing line A-A on line A-E, and creasing on dotted line.

You will have Fig. 193 B.

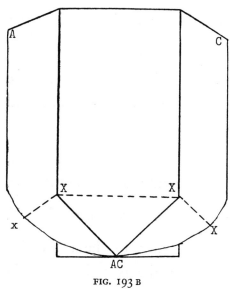

FIG. 193 B

Then crease on the dotted line X-X.

When this step is finished turn it over and repeat the directions for Figs. 193 A and 193 B on the other side.

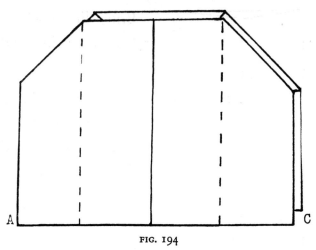

FIG. 194

Fold on the dotted lines, bringing points **A** and **C** to center line.

Turn it over and repeat the above directions to the other side.

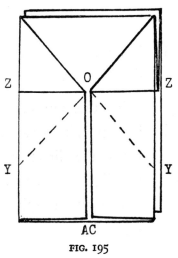

FIG. 195

Bring line C-O to line O-Z, and crease on dotted line.

Bring A-O to line O-Z, and crease on dotted line.

Then crease across Y to Y.

Turn to the other side and repeat the above directions.

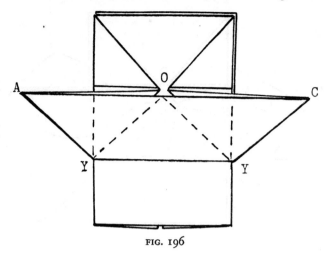

FIG. 196

Open triangle O Y A into a square. (See Fig. 197.)

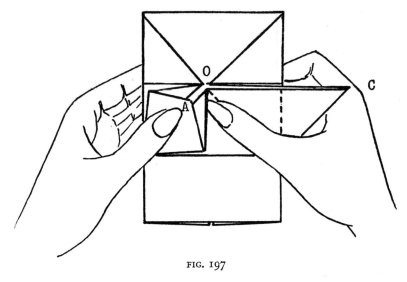

FIG. 197

Review the position of Y in Fig. 196. Open the right triangle O Y C into a square in the same way.

Then turn the model over and repeat directions for Fig. 196 and Fig. 197 to the other side.

When this step is finished, it should look as in Fig. 198.

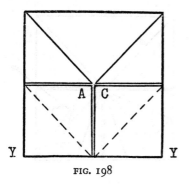

FIG. 198

Bring points A and C to points Y and crease on dotted lines.

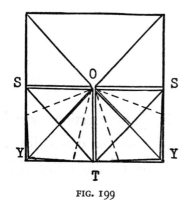

FIG. 199

Fold on the dotted lines by bringing lines O-T and O-S to the center line O-Y.

Repeat this operation on left side.

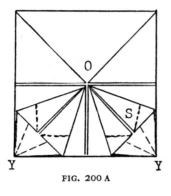

FIG. 200 A

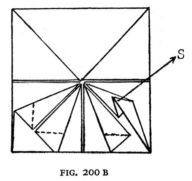

FIG. 200 B

Fold corner S on the dotted line (200 A), pushing it upward and outward when folding.

Study corner S in Fig. 200 B and fold the other three corners in the same way.

When finished, turn over and repeat directions for Figs. 198, 199 and 200, on the other side.

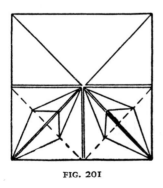

FIG. 201

Fold upper section toward back on the dotted lines. Turn to the other side and repeat.

FIG. 202

Pull little points out into position (Fig. 202).

Fold upper section downward on the dotted line.

Repeat to under section.

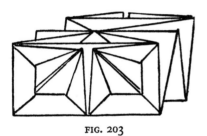

FIG. 203

To open the box, study Fig. 53.

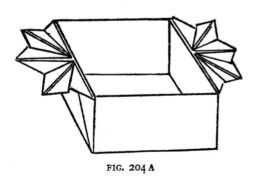

FIG. 204 A

Finished box.

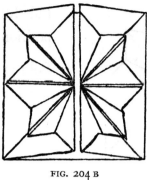

FIG. 204 B

Finished box when folded flat.

TABLE

This is a strong and attractive table that a little girl can make to order in any size to furnish her doll's house. It looks very real and pretty in wood-grained paper as well as in other colors.

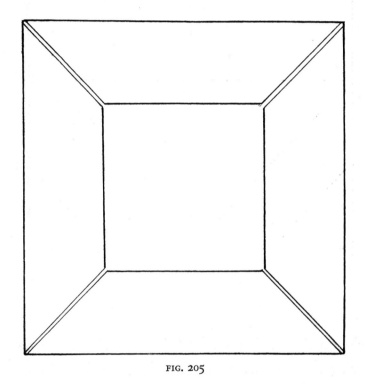

FIG. 205

Follow directions for Figs. 89, 90 and 91 to get illustration, Fig. 205.

Turn Fig. 205 over to the other side.

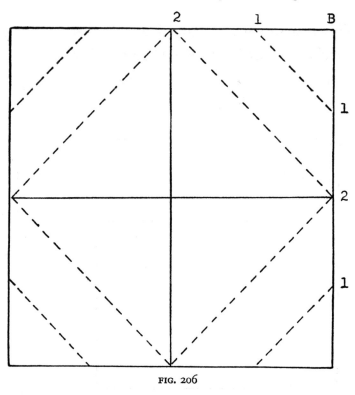

FIG. 206

Fold on dotted line 1-1 by bringing point B on dotted line 2; then roll over and fold again on dotted line 2-2. Crease firmly on the folds.

Repeat the above directions to the other three corners.

When finished it will look as shown in Fig. 207.

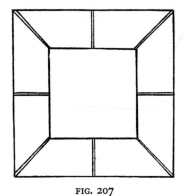

FIG. 207

Turn Fig. 207 over to the other side.

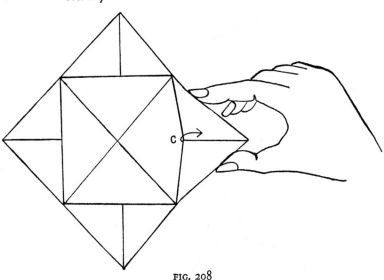

FIG. 208

Place corner between thumb and index finger as shown here (Fig. 208). Push point C upward (with left finger) and at the same time close your right thumb and index finger together. (When finished the corner will look as in Fig. 209.)

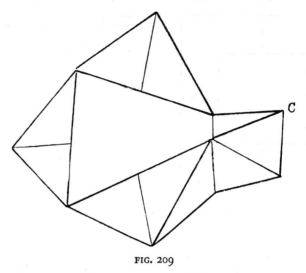

FIG. 209

Repeat directions for Fig. 208 to the other three corners.

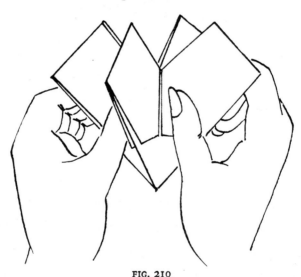

FIG. 210

Hold model in hands as shown here (Fig. 210) and carefully push the sides together until closed up flat. (See Fig. 211.)

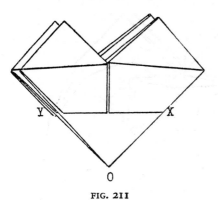

FIG. 211

Push up line X-Y and un-
fold the little hidden triangle, bringing its point
down to point O.

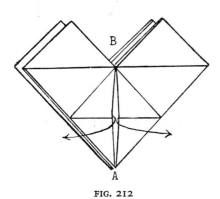

FIG. 212

Open out edges apart as
indicated by arrows, to the
left and right.

Bring point A to point B.

See illustration in Fig.
213.

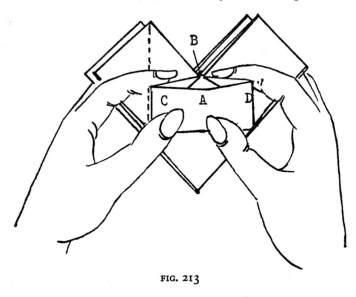

FIG. 213

Fold and crease firmly on the dotted line. Unfold. Take out corner C. Fold again.

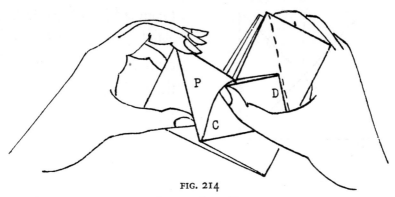

FIG. 214

Tuck corner C into the pocket P.

Fold and crease firmly on the dotted line. Unfold.

Take out corner D. Fold again.

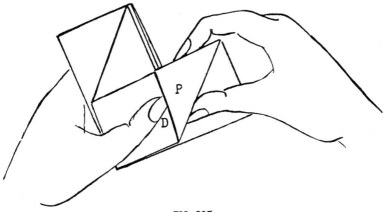

FIG. 215

Tuck corner D into pocket P.

When finished turn Fig. 215 over to the other side and repeat directions for Figs. 211, 212, 213, 214 and 215.

125

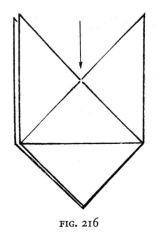

Open table where indicated by arrow. (Do it carefully so as not to break the foldings.)

Ease the table top into a square shape and crease into position.

FIG. 216

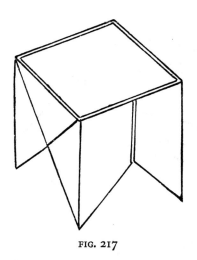

Finished table.

FIG. 217

THREE PIECE LIVING ROOM SET

It is most attractive to make these sofas with patterned or colored papers.

A square is used to make a single sofa, and a rectangle of any length, with the same width (A-B) as the square, is used for a large sofa.

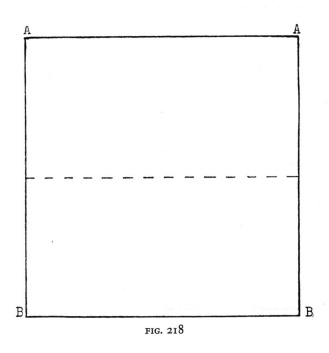

FIG. 218

Fold the paper on the dotted line, bringing line B-B to line A-A.

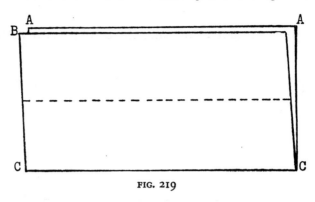

FIG. 219

Crease and fold on dotted line, bringing line B-B to line C-C. Turn over, placing C-C at top.

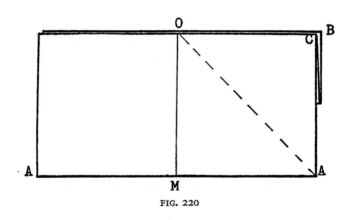

FIG. 220

Fold on the dotted line by bringing line O-C to line O-M.

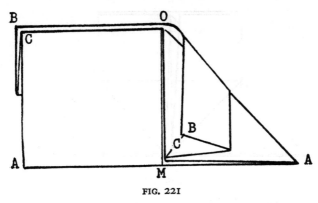

FIG. 221

Bring point B to point O and crease on the dotted line. (See Fig. 222.)

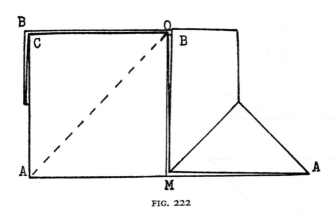

FIG. 222

Repeat directions for Fig. 220 and Fig. 221 to the left side.

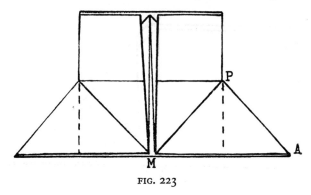

FIG. 223

Open triangle A P M into a square.

Repeat same on left side. (See position of point A in Fig. 224.)

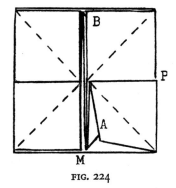

FIG. 224

Fold on the dotted lines by bringing points B and A to point P.

Repeat same on left side.

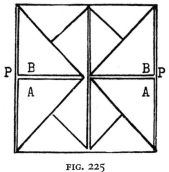

FIG. 225

Turn Fig. 225 over to the other side.

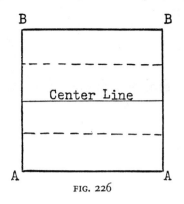

Fold on the dotted lines by bringing line B-B and line A-A to center line.

FIG. 226

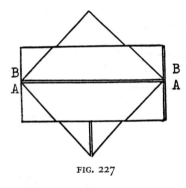

Turn Fig. 227 over to the other side.

FIG. 227

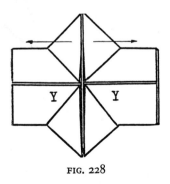

Hold flaps Y firmly. Then open the sofa as indicated by the arrows.

FIG. 228

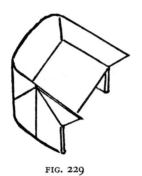

Finished single sofa.

FIG. 229

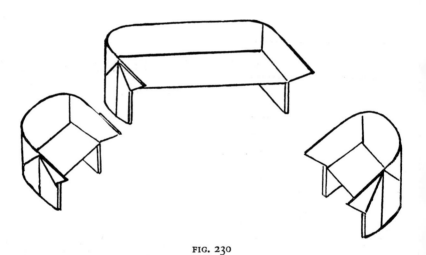

FIG. 230

The set.